55 Things You'd Better *Not* Say Around **O.J.**

© 1995 Off Color Press
All rights reserved.

Off Color Press
P.O. Box 620736
Flushing, NY 11362

Not one penny from the sale of this
book goes to O.J.'s defense fund.
We keep everything.

ISBN 0-9640362-6-6

Printed in the U.S.A.

10 9 8 7 6 5 4 3 2

55 Things You'd Better *Not* Say Around O.J.

Off Color Press
New York

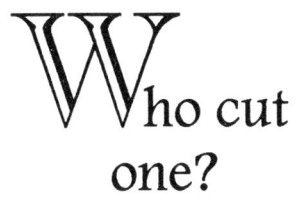

▼▼▼▼▼▼▼▼▼▼▼▼▼▼

Who cut one?

▲▲▲▲▲▲▲▲▲▲▲▲▲▲▲▲

That's not a knife.
THIS is a knife.

Have you driven a Ford lately?

Avis returned your call. They'd rather stay #2.

Urkel's playing you in the movie.

I just came here to return these glasses....

The bad news is you've been dropped by Hertz.

The good news is you've been picked up by Ginsu.

Care for a Slice?

I saw Rosey Grier talking to the *National Enquirer.*

Can you get Lyle & Erik's autographs for me?

Now where did I leave that bloody glove?

Hey *you*—
pick up
my
soap.

Can you come over for dinner, or do you have to ax your wife first?

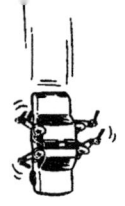

Trials are like a box of chocolates. You never know what you're gonna get.

Tonight's movie: *The Fugitive.*

Great news!
You get 50% off
your next
carpet cleaning.

If you don't
know for sure,
just take a
stab at it.

Ed McMahon just showed up with your check.

Need a caddy for that golfbag, sir?

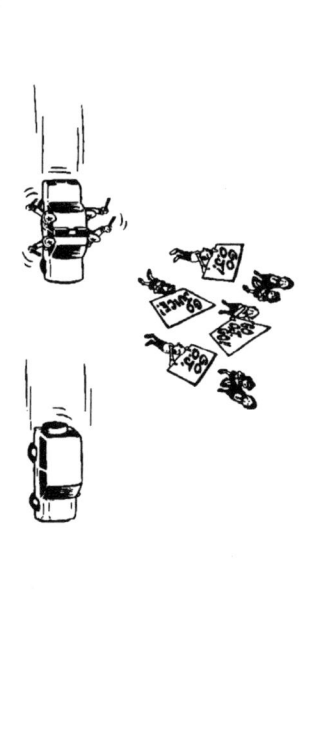

Michael Jackson called. Don't worry, he'll take care of your kids.

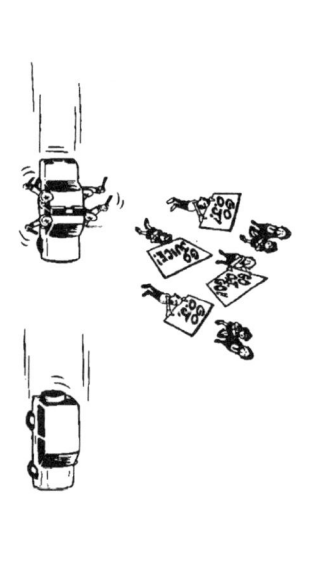

vvvvvvvvvvvvvvv

Angela called. Your guest spot is cancelled on *Murder She Wrote.*

^^^^^^^^^^^^^^^

Lorena called. Tomorrow's your conjugal visit.

Dionne called.
She sees
a chair in
your future.

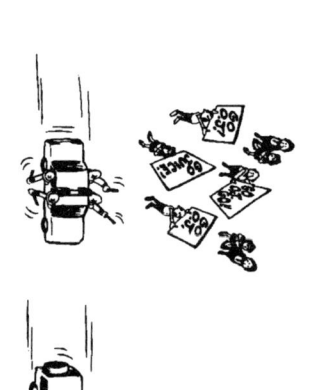

The phone company called. They cancelled your friends and family membership.

The director called. He's cut a few scenes from your movie.

Kato called. He's moving into the mansion.

Connie Chung called. She wants to talk 'just between you and me.'

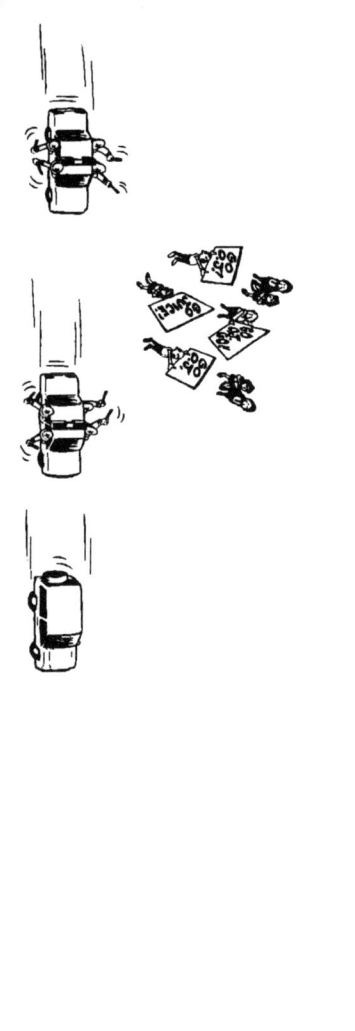

Newsweek called. You're on the next 14 covers.

Newt called. He's found a home for your kids.

Shapiro called. Your check bounced.

Prisons are full of people who are "absolutely 100% not guilty."

Do you smell gas?

They traced one of your hairs to Clarence Thomas' Coke can.

I really enjoy your show on Court TV.

This Thanksgiving, would you do the honor of carving?

The prison team needs a good tight end.

Guilty is as guilty does.

Wouldn't you love to take a stab at that prosecutor babe?

Tonight's movie: *Fatal Attraction.*

Would you autograph my copy of the *Enquirer?*

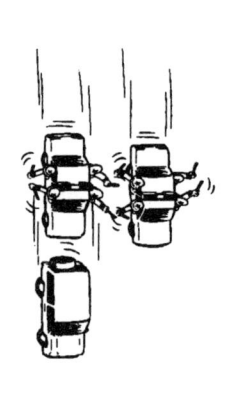

There's been a change of venue — to Mississippi.

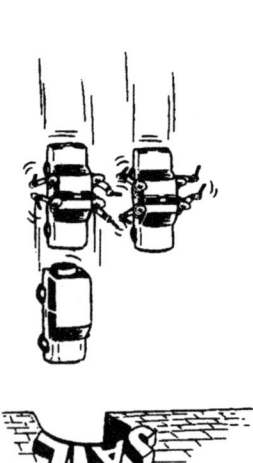

Today is the first day of the rest of your life sentence.

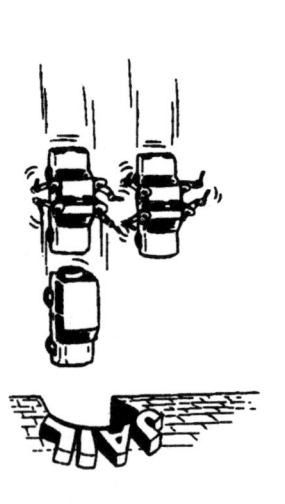

Just two more lawyers and you'll have enough for a softball team.

You can still get a job at Hertz making license plates.

Mr. Shapiro wants a few hundred extra hair samples for his own bald spot.

Love
means never
having to say
you're guilty.

Congratulations! You're on the cover of *Modern Cutlery.*

We loved your book, *I Want To Kill You.*

Your book's on the best seller list — for fiction.

The good news: Ito's forgetful. The bad news: he remembers Hiroshima.

Tonight's movie: *Deep Throat.*

You've been nominated for an Academy Award — best acting in a courtroom.

Prince Charles called.
He'd love you to meet Di.

Isn't that Shapiro we saw laughing all the way to the bank?

Your editor called. Could you rewrite the ending?